It's the wrong way to think,
but the right way to win.

LET US START OFF
BY MAKING SOME

ON THE RIGHT FOOT
WRONG DECISIONS.

A FLOP.

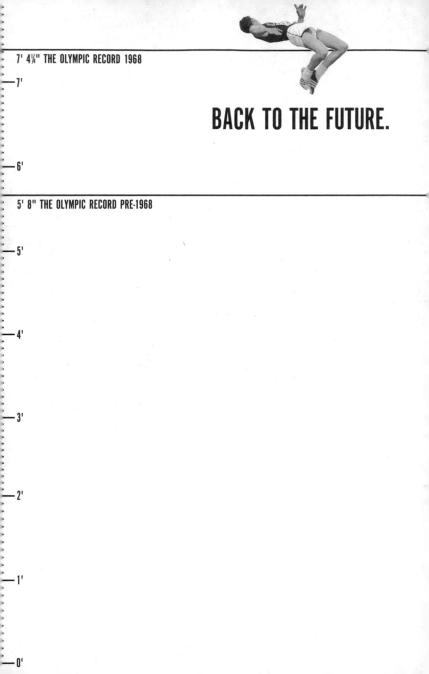

7' 4¼" THE OLYMPIC RECORD 1968

—7'

BACK TO THE FUTURE.

—6'

5' 8" THE OLYMPIC RECORD PRE-1968

—5'

—4'

—3'

—2'

—1'

—0'

UNTIL the Mexico Olympics of 1968 the customary way for a high jumper to cross the bar was with his body parallel to it, in a technique known as the Western Roll. But that was about to change.

A little-known athlete approached the bar, which was set at a world record height of 7ft 4¼ inches. He took off, but instead of turning his body towards the bar, he turned his back on it.

He brought his legs up and flipped over the bar backwards.

His name was Dick Fosbury, and his method of jumping became known as the Fosbury Flop. It is still used today.

He jumped higher than any man before, by thinking the opposite from everyone else.

This example is just a technique for thinking, but here the technique for thinking became a technique for jumping, turning a flop into a success.

PHOTOGRAPHING FLOWERS.

FIRSTLY we will pick a perfect specimen, then we will arrange it carefully, light it beautifully, and spray on some dew.

It will probably be beautiful, but only up to a point, because we have seen thousands of pretty flower pictures before.

So how are we going to make our picture memorable?

In the 1930s André Kertész took a picture of a wilted tulip. Once you have seen it, it is impossible to forget.

In a publicity shot for himself, photographer Adrian Flowers did it by showing a vase, not the flowers.

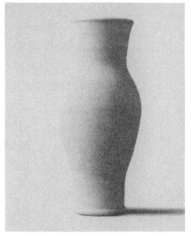

Irving Penn did it like this. Instead of shooting a perfect fresh flower, he photographed a dead flower perfectly.

Eighty years ago the scientific photographer Karl Blossfeldt took astounding pictures which were often unrecognizable. The one shown here looks more like a skyscraper than a plant.

They are all the wrong way to answer the brief, and they are all a beautiful solution to the problem.

IT WON'T FLY.

Good writers, good design and good value at sixpence.

Sounds obvious.

Not in 1934.

Booksellers told Penguin, 'If we can't make a profit on 7s 6d, how can we make one on sixpence?'

Writers thought they would lose their royalties.

Publishers would not agree to sell their titles for paperback printing.

Only Woolworths, who sold nothing over sixpence, was cooperative.

As a publishing venture it was considered a bad idea.

The founder of Penguin, Allen Lane, thought the *opposite*.

The rest is history!

WHEN IT'S RIGHT IT JUST CLICKS.

IN 1881 George Eastman, a junior clerk, left his safe job in a local bank to start a photographic company.

But here is the interesting part.

Seven years later he changed its name to 'Kodak', an odd choice since it was meaningless and in those days nobody gave random names to serious products.

Eastman's reasons for choosing the name were that it was short; that it was not open to mispronunciation; and it could not be associated with anything else.

Even today, corporations cannot think like that.

Only entrepreneurs can.

This is a painting with the Braille emboss[ed]
way you know this is by touching it. A lov[e]
opposite.

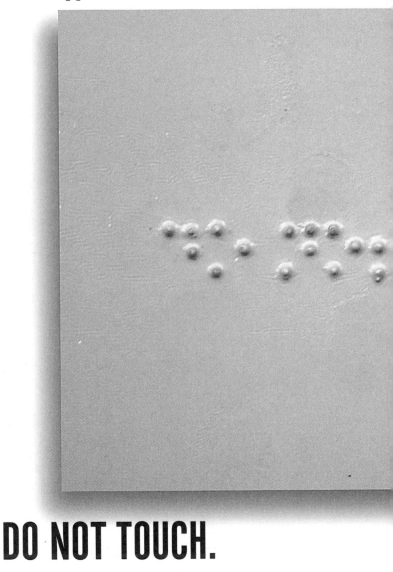

DO NOT TOUCH.

e Braille reads 'Do Not Touch', yet the only
radox, and a great example of thinking the

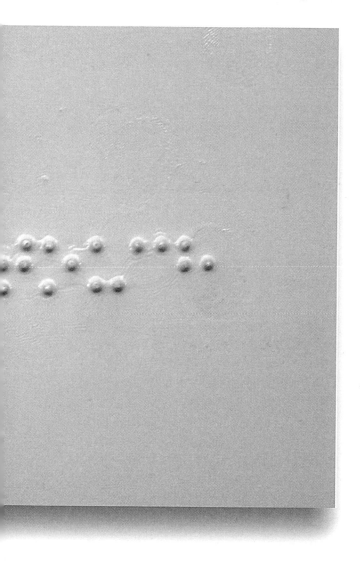

THE HEIGHT OF UNFASHION.

PEOPLE who create work that fashionable people emulate do the very opposite of what is in fashion.

They create something unfashionable, out of time, wrong.

Original ideas are created by original people, people who either through instinct or insight know the value of being different and recognize the commonplace as a dangerous place to be.

At the beginning of the 1970s Vivienne Westwood and Malcolm McLaren opened a shop in what was the then unfashionable St Christopher's Place off Oxford Street in London.

Their shop was called 'Nostalgia of Mud'. The clothes were thirty years ahead of their time. They were unwearable and unbuyable.

The shop was, to put it mildly, odd.

It closed rather quickly.

Was it a stupid thing to do, or was it a great thing to do?

Had they not been spirited and courageous enough to do that, Westwood would not have become our most revered designer, and McLaren would not have formed the Sex Pistols.

THE RIGHT EXPOSURE.

T HERE is a story of a professor who was bathing in the River Cherwell in Oxford, at a place called Parson's Pleasure, in which it was the custom to swim naked.

As the professor got out of the pool a punt of undergraduettes glided by, whereupon he grabbed his towel and wrapped it round his head.

19

TRAPPED.

I T'S NOT because you are making the wrong decisions, it's because you are making the right ones.

We try to make sensible decisions based on the facts in front of us.

The problem with making sensible decisions is that so is everyone else.

I WISH.

I WISH MEANS: wouldn't it be nice if ...

If you always make the right decision, the safe decision, the one most people make, you will be the same as everyone else.

Always wishing life was different.

I WANT.

I WANT MEANS: if I want it enough I will get it.

Getting what you want means making the decisions you need to make to get what you want.

Not the decisions those around you think you should make.

Making the safe decision is dull, predictable and leads nowhere new.

The unsafe decision causes you to think and respond in a way you hadn't thought of.

And that thought will lead to other thoughts which will help you achieve what you want.

Start taking bad decisions and it will take you to a place where others only dream of being.

IMAGINE.

EVERYONE wants an exciting life, but most people are afraid to take the bull by the horns.

So they take an easy option for an exciting life.

They live their excitement through other people.

By aligning themselves with famous rebels, a little bit of glamour rubs off on them. They imagine they're like John Lennon, Ernest Hemingway, George Best, Liam Gallagher, Lenny Bruce, Janis Joplin, Damien Hirst, Andy Warhol, etc.

The difference being, these people when faced with a decision took the outrageous one, not knowing where it might lead them, but knowing that the safe decision had danger written all over it.

25

IT'S BETTER TO REGRET WHAT YOU HAVE DONE THAN WHAT YOU HAVEN'T.

MANY people reach the age of forty, only to realize they have missed out on life.

In many cases they had everything going for them, except when the gauntlet was tossed their way, they lacked the courage to pick it up.

No one is going to cut off your right arm, take away your motorbike or put you in jail if you don't succeed.

A friend of mine whose father had links with the IRA was in a spot of bother, so he went to his father for advice.

He said, 'Dad, I'm in trouble.'

The father asked, 'Are they going to kill you?'

He said, 'Oh no, no.'

His father said, 'Son, you don't have a problem.'

Even when we want to be timid and play it safe, we should pause for a moment to imagine what we might be missing.

'IT'S THE GOAL OF EVERY ENGLISHMAN TO GET TO HIS GRAVE UNEMBARRASSED' JOHN CLEESE

A. Charlie

Y ou can't afford the house of your dreams.

That's why it is the house of your dreams.

So either find a way of getting it (you'll find the means), or be satisfied with dissatisfaction.

DECISIONS
DECISIONS
DECISIONS.

WHEN you look back there will be things you will regret.

You made the wrong decision.

Wrong.

You made the right decision.

Life is about decisions.

1. Am I going to have the practical car or the fast car?

2. Shall I go to college or get a job?

3. Will I have wine, beer or water?

Whatever decision you make is the only one you could make.

Otherwise you would make a different one.

Everything we do we choose.

So what is there to regret?

You are the person you chose to be.

THE RAW MATERIAL.

THIS man can make his body anything he wants it to be.

He may want to be a postman, a nice chap, salt of the earth with good friends.

He may want to be the manager of a shoe company.

He may want to be an actor or a film director.

He may want to be a company director with a Jaguar car and a house in the country.

Or a government minister with two Jaguars.

What this man wants, he will get.

But he has to want it enough to go about getting it.

Dreaming and talking about it won't achieve anything.

There is only one person who can determine the shape of your life. You.

Who are you going to be?

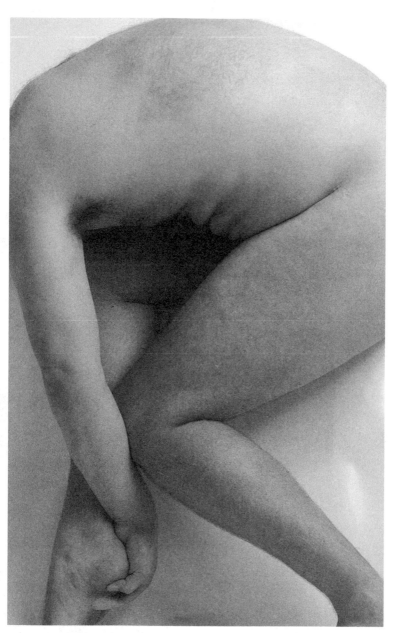

ROCK THE BOAT.

THE CASE FOR BEING RECKLESS.

WHEN we are young we jump into the pool whether we can swim or not.

We have no fear.

Either we swim or we drown.

Before the age of thirty important things happen to us which shape the rest of our lives.

The first is:

We become aware of ourselves and our own thinking. We reach the age of reason.

The second is:

In our new-found maturity we begin to think in a more adult way.

We become grown up.

Recklessness and risk are not compatible with age.

Risk becomes something which must be carefully considered.

The artist Yves Kline throws himself into the void, 1960

MEET STEADY EDDIE.

THIS CHART COMPARES THE WORKING LIFE OF THE AVERAGE
CORPORATE PERSON WITH THAT OF A MAVERICK.

EDDIE (THE CORPORATE MAN)
RECKLESS ERICA

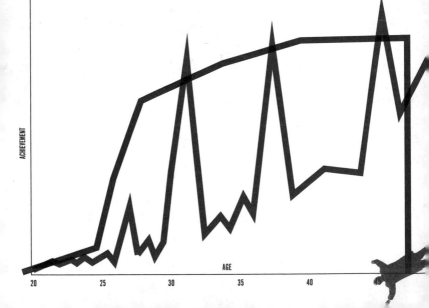

T HE CORPORATE non-risk taker rises fast on the freshness of youth; an open mind, a pleasant demeanour and good looks will accelerate this rise.

His superiors are pleased to promote him since it reflects well on them.

The candidate reaches a platform of responsibility, not something to be treated lightly.

After all he is now a manager, albeit a junior one.

His salary rises in accordance with status, not ability, and he reaches board level.

It is now time to appoint a joint or deputy managing director. Our man is considered to be a good company man, but he is a bit dull. He doesn't produce innovation: he doesn't do anything for the image of the company.

There's a very good young man in his department earning a third of his salary, who younger members of staff respond to.

Our man at forty is moved sideways, and at forty-seven he is out.

He didn't reach the top of the ladder, he has fallen and there is no climbing back.

He's finished, yet he has done nothing wrong.

That is the problem.

He's done nothing wrong.

NOW LET'S LOOK AT RECKLESS ERICA.

As a youngster she doesn't have the charm of the previous character.

Not the corporate type.

She's irritating but enthusiastic and popping with daft ideas.

So they keep her on.

Most of her ideas are regarded as impractical, too adventurous or plain silly. But somewhere in the company someone picks up one of her wilder thoughts and promotes it. It gets noticed because it is different and fresh.

For the next three years she produces a series of unusable ideas. She becomes increasingly irritating and is fired.

Now the odd thing is that it is not as difficult for her to get a new job as she thought, because a number of people remember that rather good idea she produced three years ago. They prefer to gloss over the failures.

Her name on the payroll adds a bit of glamour to her new company.

But the same process happens again. Once more she is fired, but now there are two pieces of work that make her memorable.

She's not just a one-off.

Her whole life is lived like this, a series of ups and downs, more downs than ups.

But when she reaches the age of forty she has a track record.

She has become a respected person.

Still reckless Erica, but more in demand than ever because she failed to conform.

ARE YOU BEING REASONABLE?

SALOMON BROTHERS, the well-known New York investment house, met with prospective clients not once a month or once a day, but three times a day.

That is unreasonable.

But it works.

Most people are reasonable, that's why they only do reasonably well.

George Bernard Shaw said:
'The reasonable man adapts himself to the world. The unreasonable man adapts the world to himself. All progress depends upon the unreasonable man.'

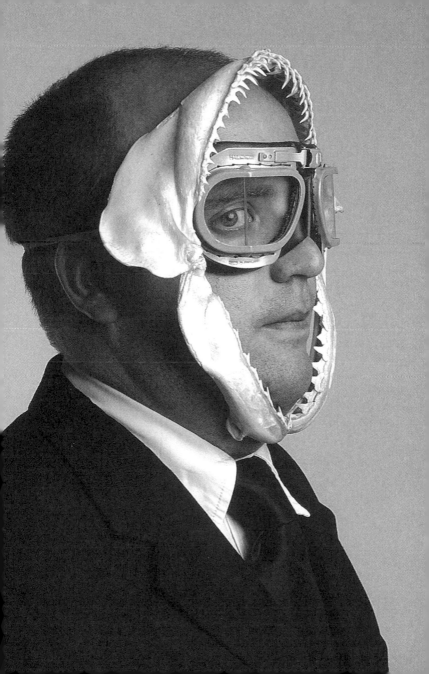

THE AGE OF UNREASON.

OLD GOLFERS don't win (it's not an absolute, it's a general rule).

Why?

The older golfer can hit the ball as far as the young one.

He chips and putts equally well.

And will probably have a better knowledge of the course.

So why does he take the extra stroke that denies him victory?

Experience.

He knows the downside, what happens if it goes wrong, which makes him more cautious.

The young player is either ignorant or reckless to caution.

That is his edge.

It is the same with all of us.

Knowledge makes us play safe.

The secret is to stay childish.

What the young can do to the old.

OVER THE TOP.

WHEN the Berlin wall was due to come down, a junior executive* of a certain advertising agency came to me with an idea for pasting a poster on the other side of the wall.

I said, 'Good idea, but where are you going to get the money from?'

He said that he had some saved up.

I said, 'How will you get it done?'

He said, 'I'll get it done.'

He did. It made worldwide news.

Needless to say, he went off to start his own company.

All the best ones do.

EVERYBODY NEEDS

ONE OF THESE.

IF you want to know how your life
is going to turn out, you just have
to know where you're heading.

REACH FOR THE STARS.

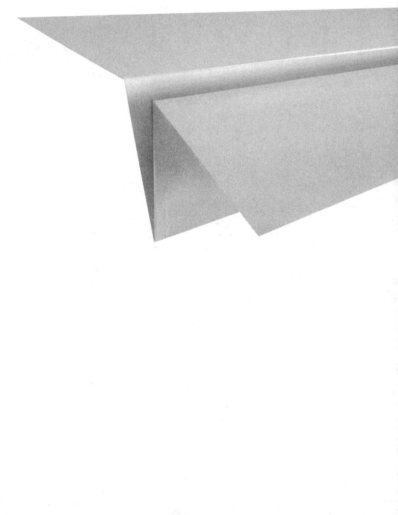

If this is the level of your ambition,

try aiming higher.

DO IT, THEN FIX IT AS YOU GO.

Too many people spend too much time trying to perfect something before they actually do it.

Instead of waiting for perfection, run with what you've got, and fix it as you go.

ASK FOR A SLAP
IN THE FACE.

IF YOU show somebody a piece of your work and you ask them 'What do you think?', they will probably say it's okay because they don't want to offend you.

Next time, instead of asking if it's right, ask them what's wrong.

They may not say what you want to hear, but the chances are they will give you a truthful criticism.

Truth hurts, but in the long run it's better than a pat on the back.

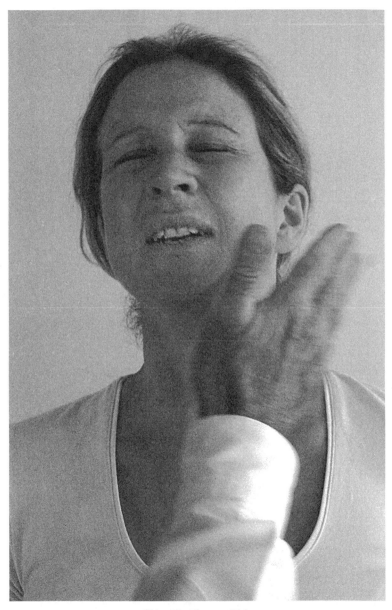

This will make you think.

TAKE CHARGE.

Be your own worst critic.

When things go wrong it's tempting to shift the blame. Don't.

Accept responsibility. People will appreciate it, and you will find out what you're capable of.

IF YOU WANT TO BE INTERESTING, BE INTERESTED.

I LEFT a friend of mine in a pub in Copenhagen; he knew only two words of Danish, *ja* and *nej* (yes and no).

A drunken man began speaking to him, and my friend interjected occasionally with a *ja* or *nej*.

When I returned later my friend was still in conversation with the drunk, still using the same two words.

The drunk found my friend to be an interesting person, simply because he listened to him.

In an interview it is better to listen carefully to what the interviewers have to say than put on a show of your own brilliance.

That way they will be interested in you without you saying a word.

CALL YOURSELF AN ARTIST.

IN the 1980s Ron Mueck was a model maker.

He made the back of the man's head (*right*) for an advertisement.

His fee was modest.

A famous art collector discovered his work.

His status changed from model maker to artist.

His work is now valued at one hundred times what it was worth.

How you present yourself is how others will value you.

Dead Dad
SCULPTURE BY RON MUECK

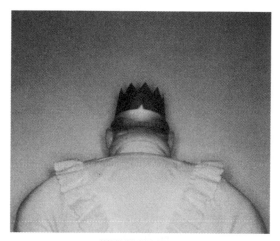

MODEL BY RON MUECK

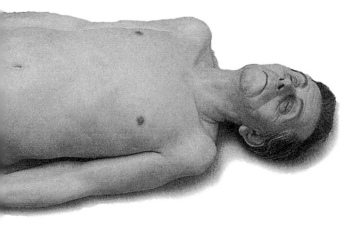

BEAT THIS.

A YOUNG man worked as a runner in an advertising firm.

One day he said to his manager, 'I'm leaving. I'm going to be a drummer.'

The manager said, 'I didn't know you played the drums.'

He replied, 'I don't, but I'm going to.'

A few years later that young man played in a band with Eric Clapton and Jack Bruce, and it was called Cream, and the young man's name was Ginger Baker.

He became what he wanted to become before he knew he could do it.

He had a goal.

ERGO EGO.

No ONE but No. 1

_____

IT IS fashionable for so-called thinking people to try to lose their ego.

Well, they should think a bit harder.

Presumably we were given egos for a reason.

Great people have great egos; maybe that's what makes them great.

So let us put it to good use rather than try to deny it.

Life's all about 'me' anyway.

MY FATHER was a modest man, and like all modest men he tried to keep his ego in check.

He did a pretty good job of it, remaining anonymous for most of his life.

He was an artist.

When my mother died, my father was ninety.

He no longer had someone to show his work to, to gain approval.

Without realizing it, he found his ego.

His work became funny, barmy and unique. He even started calling himself a genius.

I wouldn't go as far as that, but when he died all I wanted from his estate were the sketch books of his final years.

Without his ego he would never have become the man he was.

If that is what ego does for the quality of your inventiveness, I hope to further develop mine.

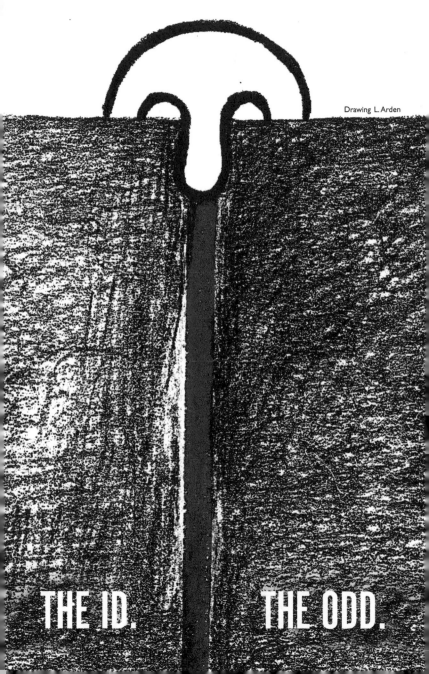

Drawing L. Arden

THE ID.　　　THE ODD.

HALF NELSON.

If Nelson had been placed on a small pedestal, would he be only half the man he is today?

FULL NELSON

MORE SHIRT-SLEEVE THAN PIN-STRIPE.

IN a meeting you don't have to worry about how you are coming across to colleagues, because they are busy worrying about how they are coming across to you.

Meetings are for those with not enough to do.

A meeting is a performance, an act to convince people of their own importance.

The real players don't need to act out the meeting game.

They roll up their sleeves and get on with the job.

If you must have a meeting, lose the chairs

WHAT'S YOUR POI

OF VIEW ?

'MOST PEOPLE ARE OTHER PEOPLE.

THEIR THOUGHTS ARE SOMEONE ELSE'S OPINIONS,

THEIR LIVES A MIMICRY,

THEIR PASSIONS A QUOTATION.' Oscar Wilde

WHAT'S YOUR OPINION?

THERE IS NO RIGHT POINT OF VIEW.

There is a conventional or popular point of view.

There is a personal point of view.

There is a large point of view which the majority share.

There is a small point of view which just a few share.

But there is no right
point of view.

You are always right.

You are always wrong.

It just depends from
which pole you are
looked at.

Advances in any field
are built upon people
with the small or
personal point of view.

LOOK AT IT THIS WAY.

GILBERT GARCIN IS 80 YEARS OLD. HE STARTED TAKING PICTURES
WHEN HE WAS 65. HE HAS A POINT OF VIEW. YOU'RE LOOKING AT IT.

I used to commission a lot of photography.

Consequently, people were keen to show me their work.

99 per cent of the portfolios I saw were of a very high standard.

But 98 per cent of them contained pictures I had seen before.

Obviously not the same subject or composition, but I had the general impression that I was not seeing anything new.

They didn't have a point of view. If they did, it was that the viewer of their pictures (me) should like their work.

Very occasionally, I saw the work of someone who did have a point of view, whose work was like no one else's.

These were often difficult people, almost unemployable because you couldn't tell them what to do.

Sometimes it went wrong.

Sometimes it didn't.

When it didn't go wrong, it more than made up for the times it did.

1984.

IN 1975 the Czech artist and animator Jan Svankmajer had his work suppressed by the communists.

Had he the wrong point of view?

Or was it the right point of view seen by the wrong people?

Today he is a national treasure.

Is he now right and they were wrong? Or is he still wrong and they were right?

It is exactly the same work, but seen from a different point of view.

The prevailing one being what the majority think.

People are like sheep: they follow the leader. It is the leader who has a point of view about which way they should go.

Having an original point of view or angle is a novelty.

Recognizing its value is intelligent.

Having the courage to stand up for it in the face of public opinion is what makes you a winner.

H.M.MMMM?

WHOSE OPINION IS SHE THINKING?

A COLLEAGUE of mine took his friend to see an art exhibition in north London.

The show was basically piles of breeze blocks forming armchair and settee shapes, painted in primary colours.

Seeing these the colleague said, 'You brought me all the way out here to see this pile of junk when we could have been having a nice lunch?' He continued his rant about the work all the way back to the office.

When they got there my friend said, 'You said you don't like the work, but you haven't stopped talking about it since you first saw it.'

Whether he liked it or not, he could not forget it.

If work is fresh and new, you can't expect to like it straightaway, because you have nothing to compare it with.

The effort of coming to terms with things you do not understand makes them all the more valuable to you when you do grasp them.

Good art speaks for itself. That doesn't mean you have to like it.

So the next time you go to an art show, or look at anything for that matter, observe what effect it has on you and try to form your own opinion.

That way you become the critic and not a mouthpiece for someone else's opinions.

TURN THIS BOOK UPSIDE DOWN.

_____

THINGS ARE LOOKING UP ALREADY.

87

WHAT IS A GOOD IDEA?

One that happens is.

If it doesn't, it isn't.

When a client asked how much it would cost to get permission to photograph the Eiffel Tower for use in an advertisement, the bureaucrats representing the City of Paris said £10,000.

The client didn't think that was such a good idea any more.

So they didn't use it.

I wanted it for this book, but I don't think £10,000 is such a good idea either.

So I didn't ask.

WHAT IS A BAD IDEA?

IDEAS are a matter of taste.

What is a good idea to some can be bad or boring to others.

A good idea is a clever solution to a problem, one that I have never seen before.

But if an idea is not taken up and used as a solution to a problem it has no value.

It becomes a non-idea.

Lying in a drawer it is useless.

Worse than useless, it's a complete waste of space.

Ideas have to be applied before they are recognized as good ideas.

Even a bad idea executed is better than a good idea undone.

The longer it is used the better the idea is considered to be.

That is why the wheel is reckoned to be the best idea ever.

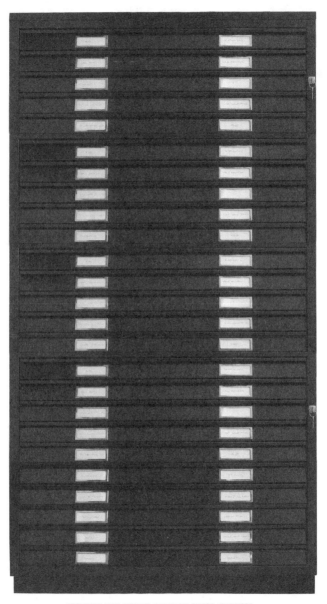

THE BEST IDEA HERE IS THE PLAN CHEST. IT EXISTS.

IT'S NOT ALWAYS GOOD TO HAVE IDEAS.

SOME people have a gift for coming up with ideas. But for those that don't it is a real struggle.

Oddly, the people who struggle most are often the ones who become the most successful.

Having too many ideas is not always a good thing.

It's too easy to move on to the next one, and the next one.

If you don't have many ideas, you have to make those you do have work for you.

WHERE TOO MANY GOOD IDEAS END UP

STEAL.

STEAL from anywhere that resonates with inspiration or fuels your imagination.

Devour films, music, books, paintings, poems, photographs, conversations, dreams, trees, architecture, street signs, clouds, light and shadows.

Select only things to steal from that speak directly to your soul. If you do this, your work (and theft) will be authentic.

Authenticity is invaluable.

Originality is non-existent.

Don't bother concealing your thievery — celebrate it if you feel like it.

Remember what Jean-Luc Godard said: '*It's not where you take things from — it's where you take them to.*'

I stole this from Jim Jarmusch

SOMETIMES THE CLEVER THIN

Take a picture of a glass, turn the camera out of focus and use a distorting lens.

Then ask people, 'What's that?'

They will answer, 'It's a picture of a glass.'

S NOT TO BE TOO CLEVER.

Take another picture of the same glass. Don't put it out of focus and don't distort it. Make it normal.

Then ask people, 'What's that?'

They will answer, 'It's a glass.'

BREAD. YOU KNOW IT MAKES SANDWICHES.

THI$ WILL MAKE YOU CREATIVE.

For a creative person starting out on a career, try not thinking about film or media or whatever.

Think about money. It's honest.

DON'T STAY TOO LONG IN A JOB.

RESIGN.
IT'S THE WAY TO SHOW YOU MEAN BUSINESS.

IF PEOPLE constantly reject your ideas or what you have to offer, resign.

You can't keep fighting and losing, that makes you a problem.

If you are good, and right for the job, your resignation will not be accepted.

You'll be re-signed, on your terms.

If they accept your resignation, you were in the wrong job, and it is better for you to move on.

It takes courage, but it is the right move.

FIRED?
IT'S THE BEST THING THAT CAN HAPPEN TO YOU.

THINGS not going too well at work?

Frightened of being fired?

Waking up at 4 a.m. worried sick?

Okay. Just imagine you were fired ten days ago.

Since you had no choice but to accept it, you might as well look upon it as a good thing.

You will have to arrange your life differently.

You hated your situation anyway.

You must begin again.

It's a wonderful opportunity for you.

Literally, they let you go.

CHURCHILL said that when you are at the top you only have to think about policies.

When you are number two you have to think about what your boss is thinking, and what your opposite number is thinking, before you begin to think about policies.

Start your own company, then you can have control of your own destiny. It makes you number one from the start.

NUMBER

UNIVERSITY CHALLENGE.

DON'T GO TO UNIVERSITY.

GOING to university usually means, 'I don't know what to do with my life, so I'll go to university.'

A gap year confirms this.

They are delaying tactics.

Some people are lucky enough to know what they want to do early in life.

The majority have great difficulty in putting their assets to useful purpose.

I feel sorry for these people. It isn't easy for them. But going to university is not going to solve their problem.

Whereas going to work will.

UNIVERSITY STUDENT
AGE TWENTY-THREE

GO TO WORK.

IF YOU start work at eighteen, you are five years ahead of someone starting at twenty-three.

At twenty-three, for all your education, you will still be the office junior.

If you get your career decisions wrong when you are young, you can alter course, but at twenty-eight it is a bit late to find out you are in the wrong job.

So don't go to university unless the subject of your learning is close to your heart.

Go to work and do your learning in the school of life.

THE SCHOOL OF LIFE
AGE TWENTY-THREE

SCHOOL
OF
THOUGHT

HERE IS A LESSON.

IT IS better to live in ignorance than with knowledge.

Solving the problem is the exciting part, not knowing the answer.

Once a conjuring trick is explained it loses its magic.

The excitement of a game of football is in not knowing who is going to be the winner.

Some people have success and rest on their laurels.

The lucky ones continue to live in ignorance.

MUM!
I'VE FAILED MY EXAMS.

DISASTER?

IT'S AN ACHIEVEMENT.

———

I**T'S** commonplace to do all right or be somewhere in the middle.

Being bottom or near the bottom has merit.

It means you are not interested in the run-of-the-mill way in which you are being taught. Your mind is elsewhere.

Fantasizing.

Many people who bottomed out at school have gone on to be rich and successful, not due to their pass marks, but because of their imagination.

So in order to succeed in your failure, you have to think of your failed situation as a good place to start from.

Good marks will not secure you an interesting life.

Your imagination will.

THE ACHIEVEMENT

OF FAILURE.

I failed to think
of an illustration
for this page.

TURN UP.

IF you don't have the degrees or fees to go to university, just turn up.

If you want to be in a job where they won't accept you, just turn up.

Go to all the lectures, run errands, make yourself useful. Let people get to know you.

Eventually they will accept you, because you are a part of their community.

They will not only respect your perseverance but will like you for it.

It may take time, a year say, but you will be in, not out.

WHEN ASKED THE SECRET OF SUCCESS, WOODY ALLEN REPLIED, 'TURN UP.'

TIPS FOR BEGINNERS.

THE C.V. TIP

Get the very best company in your chosen field onto your C.V.

Be a runner.

Work for free, if necessary.

Your future employers will be impressed.

THE P.G. TIP

Make tea.

Make it often, make it willingly.

Influential people like it.

It will give them a good opinion of you, and they will want to help you in return.

FINAL THOUGHTS.

A N INTERVIEWER with a wooden
leg said to Frank Zappa,
'With your long hair, from where I

am sitting you could be a woman.'
Frank Zappa replied, 'From where
I am sitting you could be a table.'

DON'T BE NEGATIVE ABOUT REJECTION.

WHEN I was Creative Director at Saatchi's I gave a young man a grilling for producing an underwhelming piece of work.

Later in the day, somebody told me he was in his office crying.

I went along to console him.

I said, 'Don't worry, I was useless at your age too.'

SAILS TALK.

WHAT I find interesting about the Sydney Opera House is how the architect Jørn Utzon sold his outrageous and what was then unbuildable design to Sydney's city fathers.

When presenting his plans he referred to the building as a sail.

Once the committee had the image of sails on the water, no other entrant in the architectural competition stood a chance.

He summed up his concept in one word.

Sail.

Brilliant.

THE BEST piece of advice ever given was by the art director of *Harper's Bazaar*, Alexey Brodovitch, to the young Richard Avedon, destined to become one of the world's great photographers.

The advice was simple:

'ASTONI

Bear these words in mind, and whatever you do will be creative.

WHICH SLOGAN WOULD YOU CHOOSE FOR THE V&A?

THE MUSEUM OF THE ARTS

THE ART OF THE MUSEUM

THE NEW V&A

IT'S NOT FOR BORING OLD ARTS

AN ACE CAFF WITH QUITE A NICE MUSEUM ATTACHED

YOU are the Chairman, Chief Executive, Curator or a member of the board of the V&A.

You want to get more traffic through the museum, and you want publicity to help you do it.

You are presented with the slogans opposite.

In a museum, the first question is 'Where is the loo?'

The second is 'Where is the café?'

A cup of coffee and a slice of cake can be more of a draw than the entire collection of the V&A.

A visit to a museum is an outing. It should be entertaining as well as elevating.

Curators have to conserve art, and the directors are there to serve the public, the curators and themselves.

So put yourself in their position. Which line are you going to choose?*

One which will be effective with the public, or one which preserves the dignity of the V&A?

*To her everlasting credit, Elizabeth Esteve-Coll, then Director of the V&A, chose the last line

I DON'T LIKE THIS MAN ANY MORE THAN YOU DO.

WHAT I do like is the impact his image makes on a page.

The way his picture makes us react, in the way you are reacting now.

SIMPLY CHANGE YOUR LIFE.

THE world is what *you* think of it.

So think of it differently and your life will change.

MY NEXT BOOK.

Since the beginning of mankind, more thought has gone into the understanding of God than any other subject known to man and still nobody is any wiser.

In the length of a taxi ride, *Paul Arden* explains it once and for all.

GOD EXPLAINED IN A TAXI RIDE.

THANKS.

———————

This book is for my friend and mentor
CHRISTOPHER MACARTNEY-FILGATE
The cover of this book is his idea.

I would like to give a great big hug to both of these men. They have been my right and left hand in producing this book. They have not only put the book together but have added good ideas; for example the mirror on p. 65 is Geoffrey's, and the torn page on p. 95 is Mark's. They have also provided intelligence and much-needed common sense. It has been been a pleasure to come into work with them in the morning.

I would like to thank the clever writers that I have been lucky enough to work with over the years. They have made my job easier and more fun.

In particular:

TIM MELLORS
JEFF STARK
DAVE TROTT

All of whose work appears more than once in this book.

Thanks to TONY LACEY the publisher and ZELDA TURNER the editor, who manoeuvred me into improving this book. Always positive, making brilliant suggestions as well as having the initiative to seek out unusual images.

To my agent, ANTHONY SHEIL, for his ideas and looking after me so well.

I would also like to thank NEIL SUTHERLAND, who with MARK BUCKINGHAM helped in taking many of the pictures in the book.

To SARA ELSWORTH, for her assistance and allowing me to slap her round the face on page 55. And to ANDREW CHURCHILL, who stripped off for the picture on page 33, as well as being a good sport on page 43.

To my friend ROGER KENNEDY, who cast his eye over the spreads.

To my friends and ex-colleagues at ASD LIONHEART who continue to help me willingly with my tedious requests.

To CHARLES HENDLEY for his idea on the back cover.

And to the following people who have kindly allowed me to use their images:

ADRIAN FLOWERS	p. 8
GILBERT GARCIN	pp. 25/30–31/78–9/80
STEPHEN MCDAVID	p. 27
CHARLES ARDEN	p. 29
RON MUECK	p. 60–61
MICHAEL JOSEPH	p. 77
ALISON JACKSON	p. 84
GRAHAM FINK	p. 89
ROGER KENNEDY	p. 93
KARL JENKINS	p. 103
LEE TROTT	p. 110
DAN TROLLER	p. 58

PORTFOLIO

Published by the Penguin Group
Penguin Group (USA) Inc., 375 Hudson Street, New York, New York 10014, U.S.A.

Penguin Group (Canada), 90 Eglinton Avenue East, Suite 700, Toronto, Ontario, Canada M4P 2Y3 (a division of Pearson Penguin Canada Inc.) Penguin Books Ltd, 80 Strand, London WC2R 0RL, England

Penguin Ireland, 25 St. Stephen's Green, Dublin 2, Ireland (a division of Penguin Books Ltd)

Penguin Group (Australia), 250 Camberwell Road, Camberwell, Victoria 3124, Australia (a division of Pearson Australia Group Pty Ltd)

Penguin Books India Pvt Ltd, 11 Community Centre, Panchsheel Park, New Delhi – 110 017, India

Penguin Group (NZ), cnr Airborne and Rosedale Roads, Albany, Auckland 1310, New Zealand (a division of Pearson New Zealand Ltd)

Penguin Books (South Africa) (Pty) Ltd, 24 Sturdee Avenue, Rosebank, Johannesburg 2196, South Africa

Penguin Books Ltd, Registered Offices: 80 Strand, London WC2R 0RL, England

First published in Great Britain by Penguin Books Ltd, 2006

First published in the United States of America by Portfolio, a member of Penguin Group, 2006

10 9 8 7 6 5 4 3 2 1

ISBN 1-59184-121-6
CIP data available

Printed in the United States of America

Acknowledgements
Photo of Winston Churchill reproduced with permission of Curtis Brown Ltd, London, on behalf of the Broadwater Collection.

Gilbert Garcin© Gilbert Garcin/courtesy Hooper Gallery, London and Les Filles du Calvaire, Paris, www.gilbert-garcin.com.

Dan Troller © Dan Troller.

Photograph of vase © Adrian Flowers.

Woody Allen photograph reproduced with permission of Magnum Photos.

Thanks also to Getty, Magnum, Corbis, Science and Society Picture Library, V&A Images.

Every effort has been made to trace copyright holders. The publishers will be glad to rectify in future editions any errors or omissions brought to their attention.